Ferris S. Hafford

The Revellers

A Poem

Ferris S. Hafford

The Revellers
A Poem

ISBN/EAN: 9783744651851

Printed in Europe, USA, Canada, Australia, Japan

Cover: Foto ©Thomas Meinert / pixelio.de

More available books at **www.hansebooks.com**

THE REVELLERS

A Poem,

BY F. S. HAFFORD.

COLLEGE PRESS,
HEALDSBURG, CALIFORNIA.
1893.

PREFACE.

The story of The Revellers appeared some fifty years ago in a little book of allegories published by an English clergyman. I read it with much delight in early boyhood, and I believe that many of its lessons have had a lasting influence upon my character. Some time ago while reading the book aloud to a friend I conceived the idea that I should like to cast the story in rhyme and meter. As the book was out of print and the copyright long since expired I felt free to do so, and for most of the way I have quite closely followed the original story, in a few instances I have employed even the words of the author where for a single line or more they seemed appropriate to the meter I had chosen.

In some of the closing scenes of the second and third chapters I did not wholly agree with the doctrines of the author, and there I have felt free to change the story itself, leaving out portions in pla ces or inserting whatever seemed to me more in accordance with Bible teaching.

Grown people, if I may be so fortunate as to find any among my readers, will please pardon me if I at this place give the children, for whom mainly the book is written, some points to help them in understanding the allegory. The names given to the characters in the story are easily defined and they indicate each a particular class of people.

The old man usually represents the Word, or sometimes, perhaps, a preacher of the Word. Leila means pride, Roland is fame, Florizel means flourishing or prosperous, Edith is happiness or peace, and Una is victory, Camillo means a scoffer, Theophilus a lover of God, and Hubert one bright and gay in spirit and easy to be led by others, Dromio and Antonio are the infidel and atheist, and Urban means meek and courteous. The "awful messengers" which appear toward the close of the second chapter are pestilences, wars, earthquakes, cyclones, floods, plagues, or such other calamities as Christ has said should come before his appearing. You may read about them in the second chapter of Joel.

I think the rest will be easily understood, and I may venture to say that if one soul now found among the revellers will by the reading of these lines be persuaded to join the watchers, I shall feel infinitely more repaid for the pleasant task of writing them than to know that the book had met with a large sale.

F. S. HAFFORD.

THE REVELLERS.

CHAPTER ONE.

THE WARNING VOICE.

I DREAMED of walking through a vale
    Which verdant hills surround;
There spicy odors load the gale
    And fragrant flowers abound.

There woods of every tender hue,
    And fields of living green,
And skies of crimson and of blue,—
    And in the midst was seen

A stream whose crystal waters clear
    In soft delicious flow
Made melody unto my ear
    As ever on they go

Till they were lost in shade behind
    The mountain's farthest reach.
I thought that to an earnest mind
    A lesson this might teach.

At that sweet vale's remoter end
     A stately palace stood,
Whose lamps their shining beams would send
     Afar into the wood.

Around it snowy porticoes,
     And marble pillars tall,
And flights of steps whose tops arose
     To where a stately hall

Was hung from floor to arching dome
     With festooned garlands rare,
Whose fragrance filled the spacious room
     And hung upon the air.

The time was evening's early hours,
     A soft and mellow light
Threw shadows long from graceful towers
     And told of coming night.

I lingered by the stream so blue
     That wound its shining way
Reflecting from its mirror true
     The beams of parting day.

There strange, bright birds, like shining things,
     Shot through the verdant bowers,
And insects mused with jewelled wings
     Around the heads of flowers

Which stood in wild succession there
  Along the river's brink,
And seemed to hear its rippling air,
  And of its music drink.

Far up the shady avenue,
  Above the tree-tops tall,
There opened on my wondering view
  That marble palace hall,

Whose snow-white pillars hung around
  With architectural grace
Seemed doubled in the depths profound
  Below the river's face.

No human being could I see
  In all that lovely place.
Insects and birds from tree to tree
  Did flit with pleasing grace;

And much I marvelled that so fair
  And good a place should be
For feeble, transient hosts of air;
  When suddenly I see

A reverend man from out the wood
  Come to the river's side;
Beside the rushing stream he stood
  And gazed and deeply sighed.

His hair was white as mountain snow,
   And on his furrowed brow
The weight of many years did show
   That he was aged now.

He sat down on a mossy stone
   Beneath the cooling shade
Then bowed his head in musings lone.
   As near the spot I strayed

He raised his head from off his hand
   And seemed about to rise;
I quickly said he should not stand,
   Then told him my surprise

That such a fair and lovely spot
   Secluded should remain,
And kindly asked if he could not
   It all to me explain.

A moment paused the kind old man
   And tears suffused his eye;
With awe his earnest brow I scan
   As thus he makes reply:

"Come linger here an hour with me
   Till yonder sun has set;
From what you hear and what you see
   An answer you will get."

THE WARNING VOICE.

I thanked him for his welcome kind,
    And lingered by his side,
Then asked him for his further mind—
    He thus to me replied:

" 'The Vale of Life,' this place we call,
    And yonder palace bright
'The Temple of This World,' and all
    Belongs to the Lord of Light.

"A revel will be there tonight,
    The Lord is far away,
But he'll return ere morning light
    Shall bring the coming day.

"It may be at the midnight deep,
    Or cry of early bird,
Or at the daylight's faintest peep
    When morning sounds are heard.

"And when he comes the ones who stand
    And watch for him and wait
He'll take to his own heavenly land
    To view his blest estate.

"And then this valley will become
    An empty wilderness;
And wrath and devastating doom—
    Reward of faithlessness."

The old man sighed and fixed his eye
    Upon the wandering wave;
He marked the waters hurrying by
    With meditation grave.

"And you?" I hesitating ask.
    "The Lord has placed me here
And given me the trying task
    To warn when he is near."

"But do they need a warning voice?"
    I asked in some surprise,
"When those who make the wiser choice
    Will win so great a prize?"

He answered, "It is even so
    As you will quickly see
When from the lofty temple flow
    The sounds of revelry."

I pondered deep the old man's word,
    And sat in silent mood,
When suddenly were voices heard,
    And from the shady wood

We saw two youthful figures come
    Along the springing grass;
Their eyes were toward the temple dome,
    And swiftly on they pass.

One was a tall and handsome man,
　　And walking by his side
A lady fine whose face I scan
　　Where mingled joy and pride.

Each one was dressed in purest white,
　　And round the lady's hair
There wound a wreath of roses bright,
　　And gems of lustre rare.

The youth, too, by his manner showed
　　His heart was full of pride;
His face with expectation glowed,
　　As to his friend he cried:

"See Leila, yonder is the hall;
　　Just hear the music roll;
There are the marble pillars tall,
　　We soon shall reach the goal."

Just then a burst of music fine
　　Rolled out from organ grand,
A thousand silver cressets shine
　　To light the joyous band.

"Stay, revellers, stay a moment now,"
　　The reverend old man said.
Reluctance clouds the reveller's brow,—
　　The lady bowed her head.

"Young man, and you, my lady gay,
    With garments fair and white,
Wilt heed what I, an old man, say
    About the coming night?

"The music of the revel swells,
    'Twill drown the warning sound
That of his dreadful coming tells
    Who owns this hallowed ground.

"Oh! watch and pray! be warned in time,
    Remember all the woe
And sorrow in that awful clime
    Where wickedness must go!

"'The revel will be glad tonight,
    But day will surely come!
He will appear in splendor bright
    To take His people home!"

This speech impressed the noble youth;
    His laughing eye looked grave;
He pondered deep the words of truth,
    And watched the passing wave.

Then Leila spoke, "We thank you, sir,
    Your words are kindly meant,
And many solemn thoughts you stir:
    You have a good intent;

"Yet now the evening wears away,
    We cannot linger here;
It may be at some future day
    We'll have more time to hear.

"Come, Roland, let us hasten on."
    But Roland lingered still:
"Nay, Lelia, when the night is gone
    And o'er the distant hill

" The sun shall send his beams again
    It may be all too late."
But Leila's look made very plain
    The scornful pride and hate

That filled her haughty heart.   She said:
    "'Tis but the idle tale
So often heard, that ever made
    The weak and timid pale.

"Art thou, my brave young Roland, mad?"
    The youth laughed out in glee:
"Farewell, old man, " he lightly said,
    .   " For what we hear and see

" We thank you now; some other time,
    Perhaps, we'll come again.
Lelia, do hear the music chime
    In yonder noble fane."

They passed along.   The old man eyed
      The swiftly passing stream:
" 'A more convenient time,'" he sighed,
      "Poor fools, they little dream

"How soon the Lord of Light will come
      And find them unprepared;
For wrath and devastating doom
      His righteous sword is bared."

And hardly had he spoken thus
      When from the shady wood
Were voices heard approaching us
      And soon in view there stood

A group of graceful children bright
      All talking merrily;
They, too, were clad in purest white,
      In garments fair to see.

Light sandals kept their tender feet
      From waving grasses green;
The innocence of childhood sweet
      In every face was seen.

"Now, Edith, do make haste and come;
      Why will you linger long?
The revel music has begun,
      I hear the choral song!"

"I must, I must; look, Una, now,
  Am I not beautiful
With these white lilies round my brow?
  There's many more to cull."

"O. Edith, it is tiresome,
  The music's sounding high;
The evening sun has sunk; do come;
  I shall not wait.   Good by."

But Edith still with laughing face,
  Sat down and would not stir;
The rest walked on with rapid pace,
  And would not wait for her.

"See, Una, there sits an old man
  On yonder mossy stone;
How gray his hair is, and how calm
  He looks; he's all alone.

"How I should like to speak to him."
  Thus spoke a thoughtful boy.
"No, Florizel, there is not time,"
  Said Una, "think what joy

"We miss; we shall be late I know.
  Our little Edith there—
Why does she still provoke us so
  For lilies for her hair?"

"Oh, Una there is very proud,
    She's to be crowned to-night,"
Camillo said with laughter loud,
    "She would not lose a mite

" Of time for admiration."   "Now
    I'm sure it is not so,"
Said Una, with a clouded brow,
    And face of crimson glow.

The children now drew near the stone
    And thus the old man spoke,
(In strangely soft and gentle tone
    His trembling accents broke,)

"Whither, my children, can you tell?
    And why so gaily dressed?"
"The revel, sir," said Florizel, ·
    "The revel and the feast."

He stopped, and stood with folded hands,
    And his white sandaled feet
Upon the waving grass; he scans
    Us close, with reverence meet.

"Now, Florizel," said Una, "do
    Not linger here so long."
She held her hand to shade her view
    From parting sunlight strong.

THE WARNING VOICE.

She gazed toward the marble hall;
    Camillo laughed again;
Again they heard the old man's call,
    "My children, dear, refrain

"Your eagerness a moment now,
    And heed an old man's voice."
"Oh, dear," cried one with clouded brow.
    "Hark to the music choice!"

"I'd like to hear it, if I may,"
    Said thoughtful Florizel.
"I'm placed here by the Lord of day
    With warning voice to tell

"That he'll be here by morning light
    To take his children home;
If you in revels waste the night,
    You'll meet a fearful doom."

"How shall I know when he is near?"
    Then said the listening child.
"If you are watchful you may hear
    His foot-falls on the wild."

"The music, though, may drown the sound."
    "Yea, doubtless, but my son,
Some faithful watchers will be found
    Before the night is done."

"Well now," said Una angrily,
  "I shall go on alone,"
"Oh!" cried Camillo, scoffingly,
  "I gather from his tone

"That Florizel won't come to-night,
  He's something else to do."
"Yes, I will go, if it is right,
  I wish to hear him through."

"Pray, what is all this fuss about?"
  Cried Edith's merry voice,
"What is it now makes Una pout,
  When we should all rejoice?"

"Why, Florizel won't come along;
  No revelling to-night
For fear the music and the throng
  And dazzling splendor bright

"Will spoil his pious watchfulness
  For coming Judge or King,"
Camillo said. "Why, how is this?"
  Asked Edith trembling.

The old man turned his searching eye
  Upon the lovely child,
And thus to her he made reply
  In accents soft and mild:

"My little girl, I'm here to tell
      That soon our Lord will come:
I was but warning Florizel
      To shun the sinner's doom."

Then little Edith's laughing face
      Turned grave and very pale,
As she drew near with childish grace
      To hear the old man's tale.

"'Tis only watch," the prophet said,
      Nor spoke another word.
"Dear brother," said the timid maid,
      "What is it you have heard?"

"The Lord is coming ere the day,"
      He said with solemn tone;
And haughty Una moved away
      With a complaining moan.

Then Florizel moved thoughtfully,
      And bending low his head
He thanked his friend respectfully;
      And Edith's childish tread

Again was seen in flowers wild
      That 'mong the grasses spring;
The happy, thoughtless, little child
      Forgot the coming king.

Their murmuring voices died away,
    When, coming down a glade,
Two youths were seen in garments gay.
    And by the stream they staid.

The one was grave and slightly sad
    He on the other leaned;
His friend a lighter manner had.
    A face where gladness beamed.

"Whither away, my youthful friends?"
    The fearless prophet spoke,
And on the elder one he bends
    An earnest searching look.

"The revel, father," said the one
    With light and eager air,
"Already now it has begun,
    We're longing to be there."

Upon his thoughtful friend he cast
    An anxious troubled look;
He tried to lead him quickly past:
    Again the prophet spoke:

"One moment, friends, I have a word
    That I should like to speak,
And when you have the message heard
    You may the revel seek."

"Oh, linger not, Theophilus,"—
　　Thus spoke the younger one,—
"His message would but hinder us,
　　The music has begun."

"I think I'll hear his message brief;
　　Go, Hubert, to the feast;
My soul to-night is bowed with grief;
　　I'll hear this aged priest."

"My son, the word is quickly told,—
　　Yon revellers would not hear,—
Before the sun shall light the wold
　　My Lord is coming near.

"He'll come in fiery chariot bright
　　To take his people home,
Those who in revellings waste the night
　　Will have a fearful doom."

"How shall I know when he is near?"
　　The earnest young man said,
"Shall I the rumbling chariot hear?
　　Or hear his stealthy tread?"

"Then thou must enter charily
　　Into the dance.　I fear
The sound of joyous revelry
　　Will drown your listening ear."

"The signs, sir?" asked the youth again.
    "Are foot-falls on the wild
Or chariot rumblings on the plain."
    Thus spoke the prophet mild.

"It may be at the midnight deep,
    Or cry of early bird,
Or at the daylight's faintest peep
    When morning sounds are heard."

Theopilus bowed and thanked the man,
    He seemed inclined to stay.
"I will be ready, if I can,"
    He said, and moved away.

"May all my blessings go with thee,
    My thoughtful, noble son;
Soon thou the coming King shalt see,"
    Thus spoke the aged one.

"Well, friend, and what had he to say?"
    Asked Hubert when again
His comrade joined him on the way
    Toward the marble fane.

"Nay, Hubert, now I plainly see
    You only ask to scoff;
For, since you would not stay with me,
    But hastened quickly off,

" I'm sure you do not care for these
  And other sacred things;
But most you love and seek to please
  Yourself with revellings."

" Nay, nay, Theophilus, say not so,
  You should not harshly speak;
I only ask that I may know
  The pleasure that you seek."

"He bade that I should ready be
  To meet our coming King;
He said that sounds of revelry
  Will drown the signs he'll bring."

Said Hubert, "I can truly say
  I would be ready, too,
If he shall come before the day
  Begins his course anew.

" What are the signs that we may know
  When to expect him near?
The revel I cannot forego,
  Yet his approach I fear."

" The signs are very faint I know,
  It is a thought that fills
My mind with doubt." With anxious brow
  He gazed toward the hills.

"Oh, well," said Hubert, "I've no doubt
  We shall leave off in time;
I think the revel will be out
  Before the morning chime."

"I am in doubt," the other said,
  "I fear the music loud
The flare of lights, the gay parade,
  The laughter of the crowd

"Will make me fail to hear a sound
  Foretell the coming King."
"Well, well, Theopilus, look around
  And see each pleasant thing

"That he has left us. Tell me now
  Would he have placed them here
And bade us not enjoy them? how
  Shall we know when he's near?"

Then on toward the palace fair
  The two in silence walk:
I lingered by the old man there
  To hear his further talk.

As their white garments disappeared
  Far up the winding way,
He sadly shook his silver beard
  And thus began to say:

" Yon earnest youth may ready be
  Despite the din around;
'Tis strange, indeed, as you will see,
  How many will be found. "

Scarce had he ended when again
  A band of revellers passed;
They talked in loud and joyous strain,
  And near us stopped at last.

" Ha !" shouted one past middle age,
  " It is an idle tale
That makes the weak and foolish rage
  And turns the women pale,

This vale will be a hundred years
  Just what it is tonight;
So Urban, leave your senseless fears,
  And join the revel bright."

"Well, Dromio," said he addressed,
  " I cannot now go on;
I'm filled with doubt, and sore distressed
  About the coming One."

The reveller knit his troubled brow
  With look of anxious care;
His friends, reluctant to allow
  Him still to linger there,

Then tried to drag him on; but he
    Refusing, still remained.
"Oh, if he will a loiterer be,
    And by forebodings chained,

" Then let him stay and wait awhile,"
    Said artful Dromio.
"Such foolish conduct makes me smile;
    I to the revel go."

" Urban would always hesitate,"
    Said scoffing Antonie,
" I well know what will be his fate,
    For he cares not to see

" The King approach; he just now said
    He did not wish for it;
I think he ought to hide his head
    Or he may have a fit."

" He's mad, I verily believe,"
    Replied the older one,
" How we can wait I don't perceive;
    The night will soon be gone."

And quickly Dromio moved away
    With many of the rest;
But still Antonie thought to stay
    For the reluctant guest.

The youth was standing still in doubt,
 He would no further go,
And much he seemed perplexed about
 The streamlets rapid flow.

His hand was pressed upon his brow,
 His look was agonized,
Naught cared he for the gorgeous show
 Which other revellers prized.

" Now Urban," said Antonio,
 " Pray do come on with me."
" How can I to the revel go ?
 We suddenly may see

" The King whom all should greatly fear."
 " But it can do no good
For you to still be standing here;
 Pray come to yonder wood

" And let us see that aged man
 Who sits by yonder tree.
Perhaps he can suggest a plan
 On which we can agree."

Then Urban with his comrade went
 To where the old man sat,
And gracefully his head he bent,—
 Each reveller touched his hat.

"Kind sir, I would you could persuade
 My comrade to pass on,"
Said Antonie, "please lend your aid,
 The night will soon be gone.

" Perhaps, you can remove his doubt
 And help compose his mind;
He does not know what he's about,
 But lingers still behind."

"Fair youth," the old man kindly said,
 "What is it that you fear?"
He laid his hand upon the head
 Of Urban kneeling near.

"I fear, sir," said he looking up
 Into the prophet's face,
"I should not go with yonder group
 Unto the banquet place;

"I should be watching for my Lord;
 And yet I fear to see
Him come; I've heard with righteous sword
 He'll make the wicked flee.

"Like chaff he will devour them—
 Like stubble fully dry—
Will leave them neither root nor stem.
 Now, sir, if you will try

" To aid a sinner sore distressed,
    Most grateful I will be."
His finger on his lips he pressed
    And rose from off his knee.

I heard not what the prophet said;
    Antonie left him there
And on toward the palace sped,
    While Urban knelt in prayer.

And watched the waters hurry by
    Within the gliding stream.
Now toward the marble temple I
    Seemed carried in my dream.

CHAPTER TWO

THE REVEL.

Now loud and high the music rolled
    Through marble palace hall,
And hot and faint from laden air
    A hundred odors fall;

While stately bands of revellers
    Swept up the polished stair,—
The young, the gay, the beautiful,
    The gentle, and the fair.

They all were there whom I had seen
    Beside the running brook;
There Leila with the stately step
    And haughty scornful look

Trod proudly up the pillared aisle;
    I saw her in the throng;
A hundred lamps of silver beamed
    Upon her, and a song

Of happiness and gaiety
　　Seemed bursting from her soul;
Still she preserved the haughty look
　　Which scorned alike the whole

Of that gay band of revellers with
　　The old man's warning voice.
And Roland, too, was standing there;
　　Not dancing with his choice,

But leaning 'gainst a pillar tall
　　He spoke with laughing jest
To groups of youths who gathered 'round.
　　It seemed to please them best

To hear a word from one who thought
　　Himself to be so grand.
But Una danced with Florizel;
　　She seized his willing hand,

And gaily said, "Now come on quick,
　　My feet go with the tune,
I long to dance with yonder group,
　　We shall be with them soon.

"Oh! is it not a noble sight?"
　　And 'gainst her childish face
The lilies danced. Along the floor
　　They move at rapid pace.

And Hubert, too, was in the dance:
    I saw them passing by,
Their faces lit with joyous light,
    While mirth filled every eye.

The air was laden with the scents
    Of flowers fresh and rare;
There seemed a marble avenue
    Of stately pillars fair

Which led without the palace door
    Into the darkening night
Away to hills whose purple tops
    Shone in the fading light.

I noticed figures, two or three,
    Were lingering outside:
There standing by a crystal lake
    A watcher I descried.

His anxious face was turned away
    From looking toward the hills;
And gazing on the trembling wave
    His eye with sorrow fills.

"Now, Urban, of what use is this?
    Do come and join the throng,"
Antonie spoke with chiding voice,
    "Why will you linger long?"

At first no answer Urban gave,
    But soon he raised his head,
"Antonie, I hate revelling;
    I can not come," he said.

"Oh ! ho ! I thought," the other said,
    " It was the coming King
You feared."   " Well, did I say 'twas not?"
    Asked Urban sorrowing.

" No, but I thought 'twas that which kept
    You from the revel bright."
" I wish it were," said Urban while
    He gazed into the night.

" Well I confess you are beyond
    Me," said Antonio.
Then turning round his plumed cap
    He spoke again more low.

"Then I suppose you mean you hate
    The revelling for fear
That it may drown the sounds which tell
    The king's approaching near."

" I never told you what to think,"
    Said Urban bitterly;
" Well, but you must have some return
    For all the gaiety

" You're giving up; I'd either be
     A reveller or I
Would be a watcher."   "I have no
     Enjoyment when I try,"

Said Urban full of grief and with
     One finger on his lips.
" Well I must go," said Antonie,
     And toward the hall he slips.

Outside I saw Theophilus
     Against a pillar tall,
Gazing toward the distant hills
     Which like a mighty wall

Shut in the vale.   He seemed intent
     Upon a distant sound
And by degrees he stood upright
     Forgetting all around.

" What is it ? " said a gentle voice,
     " I'm tired of the dance,
I think I'll come and stand by you
     And watch the night advance.

" Do tell me what you're looking at."
     " Edith, I think I hear—"
" Hear what ?   I think there's noise enough
     To nearly split one's ear."

"Nay, but I think I hear a sound
    Above the music's roar."
"You frighten me, Theophilus."
    And from her brow she tore

The fading garlands; with her long
    And shining locks unwound
She drew close up to him and stood
    To listen to the sound.

"Hark!" said the rapt Theophilus,
    And Edith listened long;
She heard a distant rumbling sound
    Above the choral song.

It seemed to come from far away
    Beyond the distant hill—
Beyond the line of crimson cloud
    Where twilight fluttered still.

"What is it?" said she looking up
    To her companion's face.
"It is like chariot wheels," he said,
    "Moving at rapid pace."

"Will he come in a chariot?"
    Asked Edith, turning pale,
"And will he pour out plagues in wrath
    Upon this happy vale?"

"I've heard so," said the listening youth,
    "But this sound dies away
And then, at length, returns again;
    I should not like to say

"Just what it means." He kept his eye
    Fixed on the twilight gray
Until he thought still brighter grew
    The beams of parting day.

The sounds of music, shouts of mirth,
    The marble pillared hall,
The scented air, the brilliant light—
    He now was lost to all

But that low sound upon the hills.
    "Oh, now what shall we do?"
Said Edith. "We will seek the man
    Down where the lilies grew.

"He knows about the coming King,
    And he will tell us best."
Thus spoke the youth, and Edith turned
    To join him in the quest.

"Yes, yes, do let us go at once,"
    So spake the lovely child,
And clinging to his stalwart arm
    She passed out on the wild.

" Whither away, my friends, so fast ?
   Was Hubert's eager cry;
And following upon his word
   He soon was standing by.

Theopilus stopped a moment then:
   "Hubert, there is a sound
Among the mountains, and I hear
   A rumbling o'er the ground.

" The king is surely close at hand."
   No thunderbolt from out
A cloudless evening sky, nor e'en
   A sudden murderous shout

From ambushed foe could startle more.
   His cheek turned deadly pale
As standing rooted to the ground
   He listened down the vale.

Another moment and he rushed
   In terror to the hall;
The music swelled to highest pitch,
   The merry dancer's call

To groups of friends who swiftly pass
   Them in the brilliant light;
For so the young and beautiful
   Were wasting fast the night.

There Hubert pale and trembling rushed
    In breathless haste along,—
His young voice raised to highest pitch
    Went floating o'er the throng:

"There is a sound among the hills,
    The King is close at hand!"
A thrill of sudden terror passed
    Through that voluptuous band.

An instant and each eye was turned
    On Hubert, who with fear
And shuddering stood to look without
    For King approaching near.

The dance as if by magic stopped,
    The music all was stilled;
With signs of terror and dismay
    Each revellers face was filled.

The garlands of half fading flowers
    Were flung upon the ground;
To hear the awful tidings told
    They trembling crowd around.

" I said that he was coming soon;
    I said we should not come,"
Cried Florizel to Una who
    As struck with terror dumb

Stood clinging to his trembling arm.
  "Oh dear, dear Florizel,
Where shall we fly? I'm frightened so.
  Dear brother, can you tell?

"Away with these vile flowers now,
  I hate them one and all."
And underneath her scornful feet
  Their mangled petals fall.

"Camillo, it was all your fault,"
  Said Florizel to him,
As gazing with bewildered look
  His eye seemed turning dim.

"Well, well, my friend, 'tis no use now,--"
  The youth forgot his scorn,—
"I surely thought he would not come
  Until tomorrow morn."

"Well, but," said Una, "that old man
  Said that we better might
Be looking for him any time
  Than revelling through the night."

"Well, well, don't lay the blame on me;
  We'll go to the old man
And find out what we ought to do;
  Let's profit while we can."

" Oh, no, no, no," cried Una," I
    For worlds would not go out
To hear the rumbling chariot wheels,
    The deafening trumpet shout.

" I wish the music would go on;
    Who knows where Edith is ? "
Her brother turned away his face;
    Camillo covered his.

Then nothing could exceed the fright
    And terror of the crowd;
Though some in silence heard the news,
    The most were wailing loud.

I noticed Leila standing near;
    Her lip still curled in scorn,
But in the eye that shone so bright
    An anxious look was worn.

She leaned on Roland for support:
    " I have done nothing wrong
For which the King should angry be,"
    She spoke with effort strong

To be composed, " He made this place
    That we should all enjoy
Ourselves; and though he gave to each
    His work, and bade employ

" Our time as faithful watchers here,
 Pray, who could tell the time
When to expect his near approach ?
 Just hear the music's chime,

" And see the merry dance; he placed
 All these within our way,
And why should we not revel here
 Until the dawning day ? "

She spoke and cast a haughty eye
 To her companion's face;
"Twas plain that she gained confidence
 As time passed on apace.

But Roland's sparkling eye was quenched
 Of all its lustrous hue,
And his fresh beaming face was pale
 As toward the door he threw

An anxious glance. He said," I wish
 That we had listened to
The man we saw beside the stream,
 Who told us what to do."

" Well, then, let's go to him," said she,
 " He may advise us how
To act; it may not be too late
 To hear him even now."

'Twas strange to hear her altered tone;
  How little charm the sound
Of music had for her; she gazed
  On those who thronged around

Where all terror and dismay;
  The lamps gave little light;
The moon shone on her comrade's face
  And showed its ghastly fright.   '

I saw that Urban all alone
  Amid confusion wild
Seemed undismayed; his face was calm,
  I thought he almost smiled.

And yet he seemed as much perplexed
  As he had been before;
The near approach of coming King
  No terror for him bore.

"I do not feel it as I ought,"
  He to himself confessed,
"I wonder why I'm not alarmed
  And frightened like the rest."

Theophilus soon reached the spot
  Where sat the prophet old;
He threw himself upon his knees
  And straight his story told:

"Oh, sir," he said in earnest tone,
    "The Lord is close at hand,
And all is now confusion wild
    Among the revel band.

"I come to learn what I shall do."
    The old man raised his head
And made reply, "'Tis even so,
    'Tis even as I said,

"And has he come? and shall I go
    To my long home at last
And be released from anxious watch,—
    Be bidden to the feast?"

He rose and turned toward the hills
    His almost sightless eyes,
Then lifted up his feeble hands
    Toward the starlit skies.

There passed across his aged brow
    Such look of joy and peace
As told about the near approach
    Of long-look-for release.

"But tell me," said Theophilus,
    "Pray, tell me what to do."
"Oh, do, do," cried the frightened girl,
    "We must be ready, too."

" Is all prepared ?—your garments stained
    With midnight revelling !
Back to the hall, stand at the door,
    Watch for your coming King.

" Thrice blessed will the watchers be,
    And those who stand prepared;
No thoughtless giddy reveller
    Shall in that hour be spared."

The youth no longer stood in doubt,
    But quickly he returned
To where the revel music pealed
    And lamps of silver burned.

Then what indeed was his surprise
    To find the whole had changed ?
Again around the lofty hall
    Were fresh new flowers arranged.

The lamps again were blazing high
    Whithin the lofty dome,
And back once more to join the throng
    Each reveller had come.

The look of terror and dismay
    Had flown from every face,
And quickly each again was found
    In his accustomed place.

"Why, Hubert, why again this change?"
    Asked grave Theophilus.
"Because," said Hubert, "The Alarm
    Which just now frightened us

"Has been proved nothing after all,
    The king is not at hand.
Come, lay aside your senseless fears
   · And join the revel band."

"How know you this?" the watcher asked,
    And turned his anxious eye
Toward the place where lofty hills
    Were towering to the sky.

"Because" the other said, "the sound
    Has ceased, and messengers
Have come to say that hereabout
    It frequently occurs."

This answer did not satisfy
    The thoughtful, anxious youth;
He still believed his Lord would come,
    He longed to know the truth.

"Oh there goes Una in the dance!"
    Cried Edith letting go
Of her companion's arm; "Ill go
    And join her, for I know

"'There's now no need to fear; good by,
   I'll very soon return."
"Stay, stay, light one," the young man said.
   With look of deep concern,

"Remember now the old man's word,
   'Be ready at the door.'"
"Well, well, and so I will," she said,
   "But surely one dance more

"Will not take long, and it is clear
   The King's not coming yet.
Oh, see how Una threads the dance!
   I want to join her set

"For just a little while: I know
   I shall be back in time."
She burst from him and soon her feet
   Were moving with the chime.

"What think you now, Theophilus?"
   And Hubert's smile was bland.
"I think that the alarm was right,
   The Lord is now at hand,"

The other said. "But it is false,
   And all accounted for."
"I," said his friend, "cannot see why
   In that great day and hour

"Our King should not, as heralds of
His near approaching doom,
Choose things for which we may account,
Who fear to see him come."

" But it seems hard," the other said.
"That we may not enjoy
The time in harmless sport when he
Does not need our employ."

" Hubert, you know that we must watch
And have within our hands
Our lamps; our garments free from spots
That stain the revel bands.

" Who think you of yon giddy throng
Can in a moment be
Like that, if soon our king shall come
And view their revelry?"

Hubert himself was thoughtful now:
" You are right, my friend," he said,
" But how shall we amid this throng
Perceive his stealthy tread?"

" I," said the elder one," shall stand
Close by the outer door,
And soon I think the sounds within
Will not disturb me more."

"And I will take my stand by you,"
  Said Hubert, "you are right;
I hope the king will never find
  Our comrades in their plight.

"Can we not warn them now in time?
  Edith at least will be
Persuaded to keep watch with us;
  I'll go at once and see."

Then o'er the surging, noisy throng
  He cast a rapid glance
To where he saw a childish form
  That gaily trod the dance.

Straight in he darted after her;
  Theophilus turned away,
And holding high his burning lamp
  That shed its slender ray

On those around, he took his staff
  And wedding garment white,
And moved toward the outer door
  That ope'd into the night.

He noticed Urban standing where
  He left him long before;
His face, which ever seemed perplexed
  A look of trouble wore.

His lamp he held within his hand,
    Its flame he closely eyed;
Its rays were shining faint and pure,
    His staff stood by his side.

" Friend Urban," cried Theophilus,
    " I'm going to take my stand
Close by the outer door and watch,
    The Lord is near at hand."

" Are you? " said Urban with a sigh.
    "Come with me," said his friend,
" Come take your staff and let your light
    And mine together blend."

" I dare not," said the timid one,
    " My lamp don't seem to burn;
I fear the wind will blow it out
    Whichever way I turn."

" Your lamp is trimmed and burning bright,"
    Then said the other one.
" I do not see it," Urban said,
    " I'm sure my staff is gone."

"It stands behind you," said his friend,
    " You seem quite well prepared.
I wish that all yon revellers
    Our King as greatly feared."

"O friend Theophilus!" said the youth,
    And in his face was seen
The look which deepest sorrow knows,
    And fear and anguish keen.

"I am not ready; I have tried
    How hard you cannot know
To be prepared when he shall come;
    I fear I can not go

"With him." He spoke and turned away.
    Theophilus answered not;
Indeed he knew not what to say:
    Sad seemed the unhappy lot

Of him who feared the coming King.
    And so he left him there
With head bowed down for heavy grief,
    And lips that moved in prayer.

Now midnight's deepest hour had come
    And in the revel hall
Is heard the tread of many feet,
    The merry dancer's call.

One lonely figure might be seen
    Standing within the door;
It was the noble thoughtful youth
    That we have seen before.

THE REVEL.

His little lamp was burning bright:
    Its pure and steadfast flame
The glare of all the revel lamps
    Could never put to shame.

His shadow on the door was cast,--
    Outlined distinct and keen.
It was Theophilus' manly form
    That might have there been seen.

With face turned toward the open door,
    Bent form and listening ear,
He's waiting for the coming King,
    And soon expects him near.

No one was by   he stood alone
    Apart from that bright throng:
Yet one has noticed that he stands
    Deaf to the coral song.

"See, Edith," gay Camillo said,
    With voice and look a sneer,
"Why will he stand so like a fool
    While we are dancing here?"

"Oh hush!" said gentle Florizel,
    "Who knows but he will be
Before the morning sun shall dawn
    More safe by far than we?"

And silently the children drew
　　Around the pillar near:
That quiet watcher by the door
　　Had cast a shade of fear

For what might come so suddenly:
　　And little Edith said,
" If he is right, why shall not we
　　To watch be also led ? "

" I think I will," said Florizel,
　　Though somewhat timidly,
" And gladly will I follow, too,"
　　Said Edith eagerly.

And clinging to her brother's arm
　　She started toward the door:
Camillo with a mocking air
　　Laughed louder than before.

" Why, Florizel, you're going mad,
　　What are you fearing now ? "
" I fear the King, the Lord of all,
　　Before whom angels bow,

" Will come and find me revelling.
　　Come, Edith, trim your light,
And let us leave the feast and mirth
　　Before we waste the night."

"Oh, E lith. Edith," cried the voice
    Of Hubert. "I have been
Looking about the palace long
    And nothing have I seen

"Of you; Theopilus wants you now
    To watch by yonder door."
At this Camillo turned about
    And laughed a merry roar:

"Oh, she is going very soon,
    And also Florizel;
They'll watch all night for naught I fear;
    Say, Hubert, can you tell

"What makes them do such foolish things?
    You surely will not go
And lose the dance and banqueting;
    You have more sense I know."

"Young man," 'twas Roland's voice that spoke,
    "I have been seeking you;
We need you at the banquet now,
    The rest are summoned, too.

"The lady will not go unless
    You will attend us now,
For Leila likes you much," he said,
    With archly smiling brow.

"I was going another way,"
    Said Hubert coloring up.
"Oh," said Camillo with a sneer,
    "You'll not get him to sup.

"He's going with Theophilus
    To watch by yonder door."
The boy continued still to scoff
    As he had done before.

But Roland noticed not the sneer:
    Hubert he pressed again.
"I fear I cannot go with you;
    I think I should refrain

"From banqueting and revels now;
    At least do let me go
And presently I shall return."
    But Roland said, "No, no,

"See, Leila stands and waits for you.
    Indeed you now must come
You know she very seldom cares
    To wait for any one."

Then Hubert yielded to the call;
    But to the child he said:
"Go, Edith, to Theophilus
    And watch with him instead.

"I know he is expecting you,"
  The simple Florizel
Was much perplexed at all that passed,
  And now he could not tell

Just what he ought to do himself.
  "Oh, brother, come with me,"
Said Edith, "come and let us watch,
  The King we soon may see."

Then toward the door the children start,
  To join the watchers there;
Right gladly did he welcome then
  Who shunned the tempter's snare.

And now around the banquet board
  Were brilliant revellers seen.
Delicious fruits in pyramids
  Of richest color,— green,

And gold, and purple, too, piled high
  On snow brought from the hills;
And wine was there from silver cups
  Poured out like mountain rills.

Tall crystal vases held rare flowers
  Whose heavy odors flung
Their rich perfume to sent the air
  That round the revellers hung.

The lamps in gleaming splendor shone
    In colors bright and red,
And on the joyous festal board
    Their radiant light was shed.

And rich and fine the luscious grapes
    In tempting clusters shine,
Which bursting seemed with odorous juice,—
    Just gathered from the vine.

And at the banquet Leila sat,
    And Hubert at her side;
The same proud smile was on her lip,
    Her face in whiteness vied

With lilies fair which crowned her hair.
    She now on Hubert smiled,
And with corrupting flatteries
    The youth was soon beguiled.

Now Roland's handsome, heartless face
    A look of triumph wore
To see the victim that he sought
    Entangled more and more.

" The table is not full," said one.
    Then proud Antonie laughed;
He scoffed at Hubert's troubled look
    And of the wine he quaffed.

THE REVEL.

" There are some few who still believe
    The King will surely come,"
Said Roland," and they're bound to watch
    For him to take them home.

" I should have thought the silly scare
    Of half an hour ago
Would teach such folks their righteous King
    Was coming very slow.

" Hubert, were you like all the rest,
    So prompt to take alarm ? "
Hubert confessed that he had been,
    And all the color warm

Rushed to his brow.   " I felt no fear,"
    Said she with manner proud,
" In all the strange confusion one
    Was forced to join the crowd;

" But still I felt no sign of fear.
    The signs will always fail;
I know this coming of the King
    Is but an idle tale."

" Indeed ! " said Hubert, startled at
    This strange assertion cold,
" Do you not think that he will come
    Ere morn as we've been told ? "

" No, no," said Leila, " I believe
　　Most firmly he will not;
This vale will be just what it is
　　When our names are forgot.

" So often now we've been alarmed
　　And every face has paled,
I know that naught will come of it
　　Since every sign has failed."

" But if he were to come at last,　　"
　　Said Hubert, who could not
So easily put away the fear
　　That occupied each thought.

" Well, well," said Leila, " what have I
　　To fear ? I but employ
My time about the things he left
　　For people to enjoy."

" But," answered Hubert, " Must we not
　.　Have on the garments white ?
Our staves all ready, and our lamps
　　Well filled and burning bright ? "

" Oh I have very little faith
　　That that will needful be;
How can such trifling things affect
　　The Lord of all we see ? "

And Leila drank the purple wine,
 And Hubert drank it, too,
And all the revellers drank the wine
 And more hilarious grew.

Then suddenly the outer door
 Burst open and a crowd
With faces white and terror-struck
 Leaped in and shouted loud:

"The King! the King! is now at hand!
 The King! the King! the King!"
And with their shouts and frantic cries
 The temple's arches ring.

The servants' terror was so great
 That they could scarce express
The cause of all the wild alarm
 That seemed each to possess.

A moment and the banquet scene
 Was changed; a wild alarm
Siezed every one; the revellers screamed
 At thought of sudden harm.

Wine-cups were overturned and rolled
 Among the trampling feet;
Some cowered low, some tore their hair,
 And some their bosoms beat.

Our Hubert turned as pale as death
    And clung to Leila's gown;
He started up, his frightened glance
    Went wandering up and down.

Far in the distance he could see
    Theophilus' stately form
Standing in quiet with his lamp
    To watch the coming storm.

And there were other figures, too,
    Beside the wacthers there,
Though Hubert scarcely could discern
    Just who the others were.

And now again the servants spoke:
    "The Lord is close at hand,
His awful messengers without
    Will slay the revel band."

" Who are these frightful messengers?"
    Asked Roland, in a tone
That showed him struggling with a fear
    He did not care to own.

" There ! there !" cried one with staring eyes,
    Pointing without the door.
" I can see nothing," said the youth,
    "That we've not seen before. "

Just then was heard a bitter scream,
    And Una rushing in
Seized hold of Hubert, crying out
    Above the clamorous din,

" Oh save me, save me, Hubert, dear !
    Oh save me from the foes ! "
But Hubert spoke with that weak voice
    Which faltering terror knows:

" No, Una, I've no power to save;
    There is no place to hide. "
Trembling and pale Camillo came
    And stood by Hubert's side.

He cried, " O Edith, happy child,
    Would that we all had gone
To watch with you; now you are safe
    And I am left alone. "

Again did Una's piercing cry
    Appall the hearts of all,
" Oh save me, save me, Hubert, see ! "
    She pointed down the hall.

And there in tall and awful form
    Grim figures did appèar,
And as they stepped within the room
    All faces blanched with fear.

They bore in one hand ponderous books
  That were most closely sealed,
And in the other mighty bows
  And arrows were revealed.

A flame before them withered all,
  A flame behind them burned,
They marched like mighty men of war.
  Nor right nor left they turned.

Like noise of chariots on the tops
  Of mountains did they leap,
Before them all like Eden bloomed,
  Behind a ruined heap.

At sight of them the lilies fade,
  And very strong men quake,
And distant sounds of chariot wheels
  The mighty mountains shake.

Then Roland caught a javelin up
  And hurled it at the band;
Like lightning on its way it flew
  Forth from his stalwart hand.

But though it struck the foremost one
  And pierced his body through,
He never ceased his onward course,
  And not a wound he knew.

Now all the revellers were mute
    And no one heard a sound;
Save now and then a choking sigh,
    'Twas silence all around.

On came the awful messengers,
    Their mighty bows they drew,
And quickly through the silent air
    Each shining arrow flew.

Some quivered in the vaulted roof,
    Some struck the purple fruit,
And thick and fast the missiles fell
    Among the revellers mute.

And everything the arrows touched
    Did instant wither up;
The choicest viands were destroyed
    And overturned each cup.

One arrow struck the haughty youth,—
    Struck Roland in the breast,
Just as of Leila's frightened face
    He made a careless jest.

He backward fell without a sigh
    Expiring on the ground.
A cry of terror from the crowd
    Burst forth in wailing sound.

Then suddenly the messengers
    Stopped in their swift career;
Their message they delivered brief,
    " The Lord is coming near. "

And turning round as rapidly
    They vanished as they came,—
And round about them as before
    There shone the burning flame.

The revellers were still alarmed.
    I thought that now at least
They will prepare to meet their Lord,--
    They will forsake the feast.

I turned once more to view the ones
    Who stood beside the door.
There still the quiet watchers were
    Where they had stood before.

Theophilus had heard the noise
    And sought to know the cause:
But he did never leave his post
    Nor in his purpose pause.

And little Edith, too, was there:
    To him she had drawn near,
And in her earnest watchful eye
    I saw no sign of fear.

And now a short time passed away
　　And all again was changed;
Again within the brilliant hall
　　Were banquet tables ranged.

Each reveller had resumed his place;
　　Again did music swell,
Once more the merry dancers thronged
　　Where Leila was the belle.

Forgotten now seemed Roland's death
　　And his pale form which lay
Pierced by the arrow; every lamp
　　Again sent forth its ray.

But Hubert standing there alone
　　Against a pillar tall
Seemed filled with great anxiety
　　For what should next befall.

His look of terror now had gone,
　　But still he stood in doubt,
Now gazing on the rapid dance,—
　　Now on the hills without.

And then he watched Theophilus
　　Still standing by the door.
The latter saw him. " Come, " said he,
　　" The night is almost o'er.

"The time grows short, the morning dawns,
   I've heard the cock crow twice,
The lamps do fade in dawning light,
   Now do take my advice

"And come and watch, for presently
   The King must now appear."
"I think I will, Theophilus,
   And yet I greatly fear

"There is not time; I weary am
   Of all this gayety;
I'm all disheveled, and I'm sure
   I am not fit to see

"The king in such a sorry plight;
   And I can never get
Myself prepared in time I know
   Such hinderences beset."

"Come, Hubert, come," cried Leila's voice,
   "Why stand you gazing yet?
The dance grows merry once again,
   Come, join another set.

"Do you still fear the messengers?
   They have gone far away,   .
And you'll not see them here again
   Before the dawning day.

THE REVEL.

"The morning lingers, Hubert come."
  "I fear the coming King,"
Said Hubert, "he must even now
  Be near; I know he'll bring

"Destruction to the revellers,
  He must be close at hand,
For twice the morning cock has crowed.
  I think I'll take my stand

"Among the watchers." "Foolish boy,"
  Replied the reveller,
"Hast thou not learned how empty and
  How vain these warnings are?

"But one more merry dance and then
  We all will watch awhile."
But Hubert lingered, wavering still,
  And gave no answering smile.

"Friend Hubert," said Theophilus,
  "Your lamp you ought to trim;
The Lord is coming suddenly;
  Come watch with us for him."

"Well, Hubert, well, I can not wait,"
  The haughty Leila cried,
"I'll lose the gayest part of all.
  Pray, Hubert, do decide

" To go with me.   Long have I gazed
        Through open pillars white,
But I can see no sign foretell
        The King's approach to-night.

" The night is dark, the stars still shine
        Like jewels in the dome,
And not a figure on the hills
        Remains.   Come, Hubert, come."

But Hubert, anxious, still remained
        And leaned against the post;
And Leila, chiding, turned away,
        And in the throng was lost.

While this was passing Florizel
        Had crept to Edith's side,
And anxiously he sought to watch
        Or in her shadow hide.

" Please, Edith, show me how to watch;
        I want to watch with you."
" Well, brother, you must trim your lamp,
        And change your garments, too."

" I have already trimmed my lamp,
        But 'twill not brightly burn;
The other lamps put it to shame
        Which ever way I turn."

" May be some wine drops of the feast
 Have mingled with the oil !
They will destroy the brightest light,
 The fairest garment soil."

Then Florizel withdrew apace,
 His lamp to cleanse and trim,
And fondly with their anxious eyes
 The watchers followed him.

Again I looked toward the group
 That gathered round the door;
It seemed the circle that was there
 Grew larger than before.

There stood Theophilus close to it,
 And Edith by his side,
They wait with tranquil confidence
 Whatever shall betide.

With eyes in deep attention bent
 Upon a distant hill,
With burning lamps and garments white,
 They both were standing still.

To revels and to banqueting
 They gave no thought or heed,
They knew their righteous Lord and King
 Was coming soon with speed.

A little farther in the hall
    Was Hubert standing now;
A look of deep anxiety
    Was on his troubled brow.

He turned now to Theophilus,
    Now toward the revel hall,
Where, forming at the farther end,
    He heard the dancers call.

But their appearance seemed unreal,
    Like phantoms in the night;
And when the music sounded high
    It seemed discordant quite.

But Leila, still the haughty belle,
    Kept calling him away;
Sometimes he longed to go to her.
    Sometimes he thought to stay.

Among the merrymakers now
    Was gay Camillo found,
And Florizel had started, too,
    But turning quickly round

He stood once more by Edith's side
    And in a whisper said,
"Sister, I think I'll watch with you,
    For I am much afraid."

"Do, Florizel," said she, "but oh.
　　Your garment must be changed,
Your reveller's dress will never do;
　　The King has so arranged

"That every one should wear a robe
　　Of spotless white which he
Himself provides for those who ask
　　In all humility."

"Well, presently I'll go and change."
　　"And see, dear Florizel,
You have no lamp."　"Well, what's the use
　　Of one I pray you tell?

"The revel lamps burn bright enough."
　　"Yes," said the child, "but they
Will all go out when he shall come
　　To lead us on the way."

"But, still" persisted Florizel,
　　"They now are burning bright."
And still he lingered, standing there
　　In his disordered plight.

"O Florizel, do go at once,"
　　She pleaded earnestly,
"I know there is no time to lose."
　　He left her presently

And darted off into the hall
　　Among the pillars fair;
But soon he had returned again
　　And did their vigils share.

"Theophilus," said the tremling voice
　　Of Hubert anxiously,—
"Well," said the quiet watcher, "What
　　Would you have now with me?"

"I'm frightened," said the youth.　"At what?"
　　"Why, if the tale be true
That our great king shall come in wrath
　　Before the night is through,

"We of the revel shall fare ill."
　　"There is no doubt of it,"
Theophilus said, "the revellers all
　　He'll cast into the pit."

"Yes, yes," said Hubert, "but pray tell
　　Me what I ought to do.
I cannot leave my comrades gay
　　And change my garment, too;

"I shall be laughed at, and the Lord
　　May not come after all,
And so for nothing I shall lose
　　The pleasure of the ball.

" And then suppose that he should come
 While I have gone to change
My dress, what should I do? I feel
 Disconsolate and strange.

" I know not how I ought to act,
 You, friend, are happy now,
For you have long since fixed your place:
 But I do know not how

" I should decide; so many things
 May come before the end.
My mind is sore perplexed. The dance
 I think I may attend

" Awhile, and still be back in time;
 I know not what to do,
For, while I wish to join the dance,
 I would be ready too."

Then slowly Hubert moved away;
 Theophilus was pained;
But still with steadfast purpose all
 The watchers yet remained.

Scarce half an hour had passed away,
 A ruddy crimson glow
Lit up the east and shown upon
 The lofty peaks of snow.

Again the morning cocks crew loud,
　　And standing at the door
With burning lamps and ready staves
　　I saw there were but four:

Theophilus and Edith, too,
　　And Una clad in white,
And near them trustful Florizel
　　Whose lamp was burning bright.

And outside lingering near the rest
　　Behind a pillar there
Another stood with anxious look
　　And attitude of prayer.

Still he was dressed in purest white,
　　His staff was in his hand,
And yet it seemed he dared not come
　　To join the watchers' band.

Between him and Theophilus
　　I marked a difference great;
The former started at each sound,
　　The latter was sedate

And calm as one who has his house
　　In perfect order set;
Tho' evil ones should prosper now
　　He has no cause to fret.

The place where all the watchers stood
    Now seemed profoundly still;
But at the hall's remoter end
    The weary dancers fill

The air with shouts and boisterous glee;
    Though some to sleep had gone,
And some in drunken stupor lay
    Wrapped in oblivion.

And once again the crowing cock
    Sent forth his warning cry,
And ere it ceased a mighty sound
    Was rolling through the sky.

Then Una's face turned very pale,
    And Florizel caught hold
Of Edith's dress.   He thought the sound
    The coming King foretold.

Again the mighty palace shook
    To its foundation stone.
And rolling 'mong the hills they heard
    The awful thunder's tone.

And yet no sleeper seemed to wake,
    No reveller left his seat.
At other sounds they'd been alarmed
    And started to their feet;

But this they seemed to disregard;
      But Una cried, "Oh look
Without, Theophilus, and see
      Why 'twas the palace shook."

He opened wide the palace door
      And gazed toward the hill;
The mists of early morning lay
      Around it calm and still.

The sounds without had passed away.
      " I'm weary now," said one,
" I think I'll go and rest awhile,
      For no one seems to come."

"Stay, Florizel, do stay with us:
      You know not what you do.
You revellers are in peril wild;
      I would that now I knew

"Where Hubert was.   Camillo has
      Gone past all hope I fear."
" I'm tired, too," said Una, "and
      I wish the king were here."

Then all the watchers heard a voice
      That thrilled each waiting heart.
It pierced each mind with sudden gleam
      Like hissing fiery dart:

"Let all who are unjust and vile
　　Be vile and unjust still,
And let each grovelling, filthy mind
　　Of vileness have its fill;

"But let the righteous, holy ones
　　Retain their righteousness;
For quickly now our King shall come
　　The holy ones to bless.

Now all was quiet in the hall
　　Where Hubert walked among
The pillars.   Soon he turned about
　　And then away he flung

His reveller's dress. "I'm going now,"
　　He to Theophilus said,
"I'm going now to change my robe
　　For garment white instead."

"Now I have slept quite long enough,"
　　Camillo said, "I will
Be up, the morn begins to break
　　Upon the distant hill.

"And ere the Lord shall find me here
　　And I must be gone away.
What fools those silly people are
　　To watch till dawning day.

"I have enjoyed the revel bright,
  The banquet and the dance,
I've slept and am awake again,
  And have as good a chance

"As any one to be prepared
  To meet the coming King.
I think the people all were fools
  Who lost the revelling."

But neither of the young men knew
  That it was now too late,
And that the righteous judge of all
  Had justly sealed their fate.

"Why, surely, here is morning light,"
  Said Leila, throwing down
Her dice, and starting from her couch
  She looked up with a frown.

"What folly in those silly ones
  To give up all the dance
And spend the time in watching there
  For such a meagre chance.

"The morning light is breaking now,
  And still no Lord is here;
I'm sure it was a foolish thing
  To spend the night in fear.

"I know that he will never come;
    So bring fresh oil and wine,
Let us revive the sinking lamps
    And make their splendor shine.

"With feast and mirth again we'll join
    To close the morning light;
Let us begin again, and we
    Will think it still is night."

CHAPTER THREE

THE EVERLASTING MORNING.

THEN I awoke and slept again,—
Again I saw the lovely plain,
But when I listened for the strain

Of music from the temple tall
That on the listening ear should fall
I heard no revel sounds at all.

I sought the marble palace fair,
And, searching through the moonlight air,
I saw a heap of ruins there.

I wandered by the gliding stream
That I had seen in former dream,—
I heard the owl and raven scream,

The cormorant and dragon great,
And screech-owl wild bemoan their fate,
And none of these did want her mate.

I reached that heap of ruins wild
Where once had love and beauty smiled
On noble youth and lovely child.

A wild rose scrambled o'er the wall
Where lay the marble pillars tall
That stood beside the entrance hall;

And its reflection, soft and white,
From placid waters still and bright,
Shone clearly on my wondering sight.

Each buried shaft and broken stone,
Pillar and architrave o'erthrown
Were there in wild confusion strown.

Insects passed by with noiseless flight
And soon had vanished from my sight
Lost in the shades of deepest night.

I stopped to gaze.   There was the hall
Where Leila planned the brilliant ball,
And Hubert listened to her call.

There did each quiet watcher stand
Prepared with lamp and staff in hand
For journey to the better land.

While thus I mused I heard a sound
Which made me start and look around,
And seated on a stone I found

The same old man I'd seen before
The same deep, thoughtful look he wore,
His hair seemed whiter than of yore.

As I approached he heard a stir
Of leaves; he looked at me. "Oh, sir,"
Said I, "where are the ones who were

"Within the palace when it stood
In former splendor? If I could
I'd learn of them: I know I should

"Be greatly pleased to hear you tell
Of those I learned to love so well,—
Theophilus and Florizel,

"And others, too, who spent the night
In watching in their garments white,
And kept their small lamps burning bright."

Said he, "They all have passed away;
The night soon past, at dawning day
The King had taken all away."

He paused a moment and a sigh
Escaped him; from his aged eye
A tear stole forth; again did I

Request that he would tell me all
About the scene that did befall
Those who were at the revel hall.

" The scene," he said, " was very strange;
There came an unexpected change
O'er all the earth; the mountain range

" Did shake and tremble mightily,—
Great rocks were rent,— the roaring sea
Cast o'er the land its wild debris.

" Then every island fled away,—
The graves were opened,— those who lay
For ages now came forth; the day

" Was one of terror passing great
For those who had not cared to wait
To meet the King in his estate.

" He came upon a great white cloud,
Which soon became a shining crowd
Of angels who before him bowed.

" O'er him a glowing rainbow spread,
A golden crown was on his head,
And in his hand a sickle red.

" Then gazing toward the palace I
Heard the exceeding bitter cry
Of one in greatest agony. ,

" Then men from out the palace door
A form like haughty Leila's bore;
The revel garments that she wore

" When brought to light seemed stained and rent;
The night in revels she had spent
And now a bitter cry she sent

" Which pierced the hearts of all who heard.
Then stern and awful forms appeared,
Whose presence all the revellers feared.

" They seized her, heeding not her cry.
She begged that they would let her try
Once more; but still they swiftly fly.

" And now she cursed her haughty pride,
And called on rocks and hills to hide
Or crush her in their caverns wide.

" These heeded not how sore she wept,
But each its own foundation kept,—
In everlasting silence slept.

"She called unto the palace tall,
And begged that it might crumbling fall
And bury neath its massive wall

" Her guilty head; but still it stood
In silence there.   No one now could
Save or assist her if he would.

" 'Twas very piteous to hear
Her agonizing cries of fear
When there was none to help her near.

" Repentance came, but all too late.
Oh! sadly she bemoaned her fate,
And sore bewailed her lost estate.

" I heard her cry, ' I am undone !
Oh me ! my brief probation's run.
My punishment has now begun. ' "

" Where did they take her then ? " asked I.
" I did not see," he made reply,
" Somewhere among the mountains high.

" I could not follow that swift flight.
They soon had passed beyond my sight,
And all were lost in shades of night.

" But I doubt not they left her there
To perish in her mad despair;
For, borne upon the chilling air,

" I heard a voice which seemed to say,
' Now let her there in silence stay
Till second resurrection day.' "

" Please tell me of Camillo, too,"
Said I, " the one who scoffed at you
And revelled all the long night through."

" Ah, yes ! " said he, " he scoffed no more,
His bitter smile of scorn was o'er,
He hurried to the palace door

"To find the way to where he laid
His staff and garments when he made
His choice to join the gay parade.

"But he could never find the place.
Once and again he would retrace
His wandering steps; his anxious face

"Grew dark with terror and dismay.
He could by no means find the way;
But evermore he seemed to stray

"From post to post.   He thought he knew
Quite well the hall; but hastening through
Its rooms and doors, the wild wind blew

"Each revel lamp, till all was dark,
And not a thing remained to mark
The way; but staring wild and stark

"He groaned in great despair.   Those who
Saw him say that the poor boy knew
Not where he was, but ever grew

"Still more perplexed.   At every turn
He cried aloud that he might learn
The way he sought.   In deep concern

"He cried, 'Oh, who will show me now
Where I may find my lamp? I know
Not where to look; will no one show

" ' Me where I left my garment white ? '
And then he ran with all his might
To seek some refuge from his fright.

" But no one heeded his despair,
Nor his shrill cries that rent the air.
Now all too late his bitter prayer

" Was heard.   At length the messengers
Of vengence see him.   Now occurs
Another scene,——his fate like hers   •

" I saw before,——toward the hill
Where Leila was they went until
They shut him up, and all was still. "

" Indeed," said I, " what thou hast told
Doth make my very blood run cold.
Now, sir, if I am not too bold,

" I wish that I might learn of those
Who heard thy warning and who chose
To leave the revel ere its close. "

Then his eye kindled at the thought
Of memories which my question brought,
And for a time it seemed he sought

For words in which he could express
The state of untold happiness
In those the King had deigned to bless.

"Oh would I could," he said, "find word
To tell what rapturous feelings stirred
The ones who waited for their Lord!

"Theophilus, and Una, too,
And Florizel, and Edith who
Had watched for him the long night through.

"I saw them, sir, from where I stood
Below the palace in the wood.
My mind was in its saddest mood,

"For I had viewed with deep concern
These strange, wild scenes.   At length I turn
To see what further I can learn

"About the rest.   Just as my ear
Did sounds of heavenly music hear,
The morning sun did bright appear

"Above the mountain tops.   It shone
Full on the temple's guilded dome,
Reflected from each polished stone.

"Forth from the pillared portico
A train set out; the dazzling glow
Of their bright garments none can know

"Who have not seen the like; the light
Of day did seem as darkest night;
My old eyes dazzled with the sight

" In such degree I looked away;
But oh, how glad I am to say
I was allowed to see that day!

" First came the messengers so bright.
E ich one was clad in dazzling white,
And each prepared for heavenly flight.

" Each bore a harp within his hand;
And, touching each melodious strand,
Such music floated o'er the land

"As made the tears in torrents flow
Down these old withered cheeks; I know
Not why. The music seemed to go

" Along the margin of the stream
Until the very birds did seem
To listen as if in a dream.

" I can not tell you in a word
Of all the lovely things I heard
From those who wait upon their Lord.

" The train of bright ones was so long,—
So great the numbers of that throng,—
So many measures to their song,

" I thought the end would never come.
No mortal man could count the sum
Of those who led the watchers home.

" And when the long and shining train
Had passed beyond the valley's plain
I saw them issue forth again

" Beyond the hills in fields of light,—
In plains whose dazzling splendor bright
Shall never know the shades of night.

" Then came the watcher's happy band:
Each bore a palm-branch in his hand,
And sang the songs of Canaan's land.

" Theophilus was the first who came,—
His garment was like shining flame,—
On it I saw his own new name.

" A golden crown was on his brow,—
His face did like an angel's glow,—
And he could no more sorrow know.

" He slowly left the pillared hall,—
The place where he had watched tho' all
Had left him for the brilliant ball,—

" And as he looked upon the gleam
Of shining ones, and saw the beam .
Of their bright light, and heard the stream

" Of music that now filled his soul
And led him to the shining goal
Where sunlit waters ceaseless roll,—

" He seemed to feel such perfect peace, —
Such joy at his long-sought release,
As did my wonder much increase.

" I stood there gazing at him long
And listening to his victor's song
While following that shining throng.

" There was such rapture and repose
In his calm eye as only those
Can know who watch until the close

" Of earth's dark night. It seemed to me
As if all nature did agree
To furnish heavenly melody.

" Not only did the angels sing,
But all around there seemed to spring
Up softly from the wandering

" Blue water, and the golden trees,
The crimson sky, the trembling breeze,
The most exquisite harmonies.

" And all in unison declare,
' How blessed all the watchers are
And every one who doth prepare

" To meet his Lord. Now he has come
To take them to their glorious home
Where they in fields of light shall roam.' "

The old man paused.   "Indeed," said I,
" I wonder that all do try
To win such pleasure, by and by."

" ' Tis strange that more do not," said he.
Again I spoke, " Pray do tell me
What was the last that you could see."

" I fancied that I saw the fold
Of his white garment as it rolled
Beyond the hills; but now, behold,

" My mind was occupied with those
Who like Theophilus had chose
To watch until the brief night's close.

" Edith and Una, hand in hand,
Came next; they too had joined the band
That journeyed to the happy land.

" Do you remember them ? "   " Quite well;
The ones who stopped to hear you tell
The warning words to Florizel."

" The same, " he said, "each sweet child wore
A crown of gold, and each one bore
A palm-branch fair,—they seemed no more

" A part of earth: so full of light
And peace purity,— so bright
Each countenance, and such delight

" Each felt, that, bursting forth in song,
They followed that bright angel throng,
As their bright garments swept along

" I thought, 'They ne'er will weep again,
But free from sorrow, free from pain,
Eternal riches they shall gain.'

" I longed to follow them and gaze
On what they saw, as they would raise
Their eyes and smile in rapt amaze.

" Just as they crossed the threshold all
Behind them in the palace hall,
And all around them, from the tall

" Tree-tops, to every flower and spear
Of grass that grew around so near
The stream, spoke words I loved to hear.

" 'Well done,' said they, 'now enter ye
Into the joy of him who'll be
Your king throughout eternity.'

" How glad I was to hear that sound !
And as their garments swept the ground,
And in the long procession wound,

" I longed to mark upon the sod
The place their blessed footsteps trod
While journeying to meet their God.

"Young Florizel now followed them,—
Upon his brow a diadem
And bells upon his garment's hem.

"As happy as a lamb in spring,—
Like pure white roses just opening,—
Like pearl within a shining ring.

"But oh ! the vision that came now,—
Such change I saw on Urban's brow
I longed his happiness to know.

"Do you remember how he stood
Before us in the shady wood
And knit his brow in anxious mood?

"Well, sir, that look no more was seen,
But in its stead smile so serene,—
So placid, full of peace, I ween

"No one ere saw the like before.
A palm-branch in his hand he bore,
And such a look of joy he wore—

"He seemed unable to express
The joy that now had come to bless
His watching with such great success.

"Oh, yes, the look of doubt which he
Once had was gone, uncertainty
Into intense reality

" Was changed; anxiety to rest.
So greatly was the watcher blessed
His rapture could not be expressed.

" And as he crossed the threshold there
Was borne upon the perfumed air
A voice that seemed an answered prayer.

" It seemed to say, ' Go now in peace,
From vigils thou art now released,
And thou art bidden to the feast. '

" 'Go now in peace,' oh blessed word !
What rapture will this voice afford
To those who wait upon their Lord !

" So long as I could see him still
I watched the happy band until
They passed beyond the distant hill.

" Indeed by looking close you might
Have caught a momentary sight
Of those they meet in fields of light.

" 'Twas there a gorgeous city shone
With light from each foundation stone
Whose radiant splendors are unknown.

" And as I caught one distant gleam
Of lights that from its mansions stream
How poor did all the revel seem !

"And now there was a sudden sound
Which made me start and look around,
And all about this place I found

" The heap of ruin that you see.
So altered was the scene to me
Who knew each path, each flower, and tree

" That I have found it hard to trace
Even the threshold of the place,
The great earthquake did so efface

" All former splendor.   When the last
Of that bright band had safely passed
It dissappeared.   But here is cast

" My lot.   To me 'tis hallowed ground.
Until I hear the welcome sound
To go, I must be faithful found.

" But now I love to wander here
Among the fragments old and sear,
And often to my listening ear

" I hear the sound of voices wild,
Or fancy I can see some child
That once among the revellers smiled.

" In moonlight visions oft' I see
Theophilus as he used to be,—
A watcher through the revelry.

" See Edith leave the brilliant ball,
See Urban standing by the hall
And heeding not the music's call.

" The revel now has passed away;
No longer do the young and gay
Sweep through the hall in brilliant play;

" But deeper far than I can tell,
Like tones of some great solemn bell,
There comes a voice whose echoes swell

" Upon my heart. It seems to say,
Those blessed ones who watch and pray
Shall some day see a brighter day.'"

The good man paused; his tale was told;
And tears he could no longer hold
Down his old cheeks in torrents rolled.

He bowed his head as if to pray,
And, feeling he'd no more to say,
I turned around and walked away.

My heart was full; I longed to be
Like those who shunned the revelry
And won eternal victory.

And I determined that I, too,
Would watch for him e'en though I knew
No feast or mirth the long night through.